I0820943

CITIZEN SCIENCE PROJECTS

Amphibian Projects

BY IB LARSEN

Kids Core

An Imprint of Abdo Publishing
abdobooks.com

abdobooks.com

Printed in the United States of America, North Mankato, Minnesota.
102025
012026

Cover Photo: imageBROKER/Farina Grassmann/Getty Images
Interior Photos: Shutterstock Images, 4–5, 6, 18, 20–21, 23, 26, 28 (top), 29 (top), 29 (bottom); Simone Ha/Shutterstock Images, 9; Alena Ozerova/Shutterstock Images, 10; Maywand Khan/Shutterstock Images, 12–13; Joe McDonald/Shutterstock Images, 14; Mark F. Lotterhand/Shutterstock Images, 17; Matt Jeppson/Shutterstock Images, 24; Jordan Kercheff/Shutterstock Images, 28 (bottom)

Editors: Rebecca Higgins and Trudy Becker
Series Designer: Marley Richmond

Library of Congress Control Number: 2025939254

Publisher's Cataloging-in-Publication Data

Names: Larsen, Ib, author.
Title: Amphibian projects / by Ib Larsen
Description: Minneapolis, Minnesota: Abdo Publishing, 2026 | Series: Citizen science projects | Includes online resources and index.
Identifiers: ISBN 9781098298531 (lib. bdg.) | ISBN 9798384932338 (ebook)
Subjects: LCSH: Science projects--Juvenile literature. | Field experiments--Juvenile literature. | Amphibians--Juvenile literature. | Zoology--Experiments--Juvenile literature. | Herpetology--Juvenile literature. | Ecology--Experiments--Juvenile literature. | Ecological science --Juvenile literature.
Classification: DDC 507.8--dc23

CONTENTS

Some marshes and swamps cover many miles of land.

CHAPTER 1

Recording Ribbits

It was a warm summer evening. Violet and her mother sat by the marsh on the edge of town. The two were listening for frog and toad **mating calls**.

Frogs and toads are known for their sounds. Sometimes the noises sound like singing.

When some frogs make calls, their throat pouches puff out.

Other times, they *ribbit*. Frogs and toads usually make these noises to attract mates. On summer nights, frog **habitats** can be very noisy places.

Violet could hear a few frogs croaking. But it was mostly quiet. Then the sky darkened. Soon, the mating calls grew louder. Frogs were all around them!

Violet's mother took out her phone. She started to record the frogs' sounds. The pair listened closely to the mating calls. They recognized some sounds. One sounded like a low croak. Another sounded like a high whistle.

They listened for a few more minutes. Then it was time to take notes. Violet wrote in her notebook as her mother spoke. She jotted down the town's name. She noted the time and date.

What Are Amphibians?

Amphibians are a kind of vertebrate. Vertebrates are animals with backbones. Most amphibians can live both in water and on land. Many return to the water to lay eggs. Frogs and toads are amphibians. So are salamanders and newts.

Finally, Violet wrote down the details of the calls they heard. She noted the names of the frogs and toads whose calls they knew. Violet and her mother were ready to submit their information. They would upload it to FrogWatch USA.

What Is Citizen Science?

FrogWatch USA is a citizen science project. A citizen science project is a team effort between professional scientists and volunteers. It takes a lot of time to gather **data**. Scientists can't do it alone. They invite regular people, or citizen scientists, to help.

For FrogWatch USA, volunteers write down what frogs and toads they hear. They do the project in the evenings between February

Frog calls can reach long distances. Some can be heard from a mile (1.6 km) away.

and August. Then scientists use the data. It helps them understand the health of different habitats. If there are lots of frogs, that means the habitat can support many living things. Few or no frogs could mean that there is a problem.

Spring and summer are the best times to listen for frog calls. But some frogs call all year round.

The water may be dirty. Or the area may be too noisy.

There are citizen science projects on many different subjects. Several projects study amphibians. FrogWatch USA focuses on frogs and toads. Other amphibian projects focus on salamanders. One project studies the spring ponds that some amphibians call home. Citizen scientists make these projects successful. They help both scientists and amphibians.

Sarah Edmunds's first citizen science project was FrogWatch USA. Now she has a master's degree in biology. In an interview, she said:

> Citizen science is for everybody. You can have no experience and they train you in everything you need. Whatever project it is, they'll give you all the resources you need, and it's a lot of fun.

Source: "Why Citizen Science—Sarah Edmunds." *PBS*, n.d., pbs.org. Accessed 18 Apr. 2025.

What's the Big Idea?

Read this quote carefully. What is its main idea? Explain how the main idea is supported by details.

Tree frogs can blend in with plants thanks to their color.

Vernal Pools

Amphibians live in many kinds of habitats. They **thrive** in moist places. Swamps and rainforests are home to many amphibians. So are rivers and streams.

Vernal pools are homes for some amphibians. These pools are small, shallow ponds.

Most vernal pools are less than 3 feet (1 m) deep.

They form in the spring. Rain and melting snow fill up the pools. Living things move into these pools. Then the pools dry up in the summer.

Human activities can disturb or destroy vernal pools. People do not always consider these pools when deciding where to build. Some amphibians travel to vernal pools to lay eggs. They rely on these pools. When vernal pools are harmed, so are amphibians.

Protecting Vernal Pools

One citizen science project is dedicated to protecting vernal pools. It is called the Vernal Pool Project. It sends volunteers to vernal pools across southwestern New Hampshire in the United States. This region is home to hundreds of known vernal pools. There may be even more that scientists do not know about.

Citizen scientists collect lots of data on vernal pools for the project. For example, volunteers record the location and size of pools they see.

Volunteers note the kinds of amphibians that live there as well.

The project also asks citizen scientists to look for egg masses. Some amphibians lay these large clumps of eggs in pools. Before leaving a pool, volunteers take a photograph of at least one egg mass if they see any. They also take photographs of the pools themselves.

Laying Eggs

Some animals, including most birds, lay only a few eggs at a time. However, many amphibians lay lots of eggs at a time. In fact, some frogs and toads can lay thousands of eggs at once. This raises the chances that some of their offspring will survive.

Salamander eggs are often attached to rocks or sticks under the water.

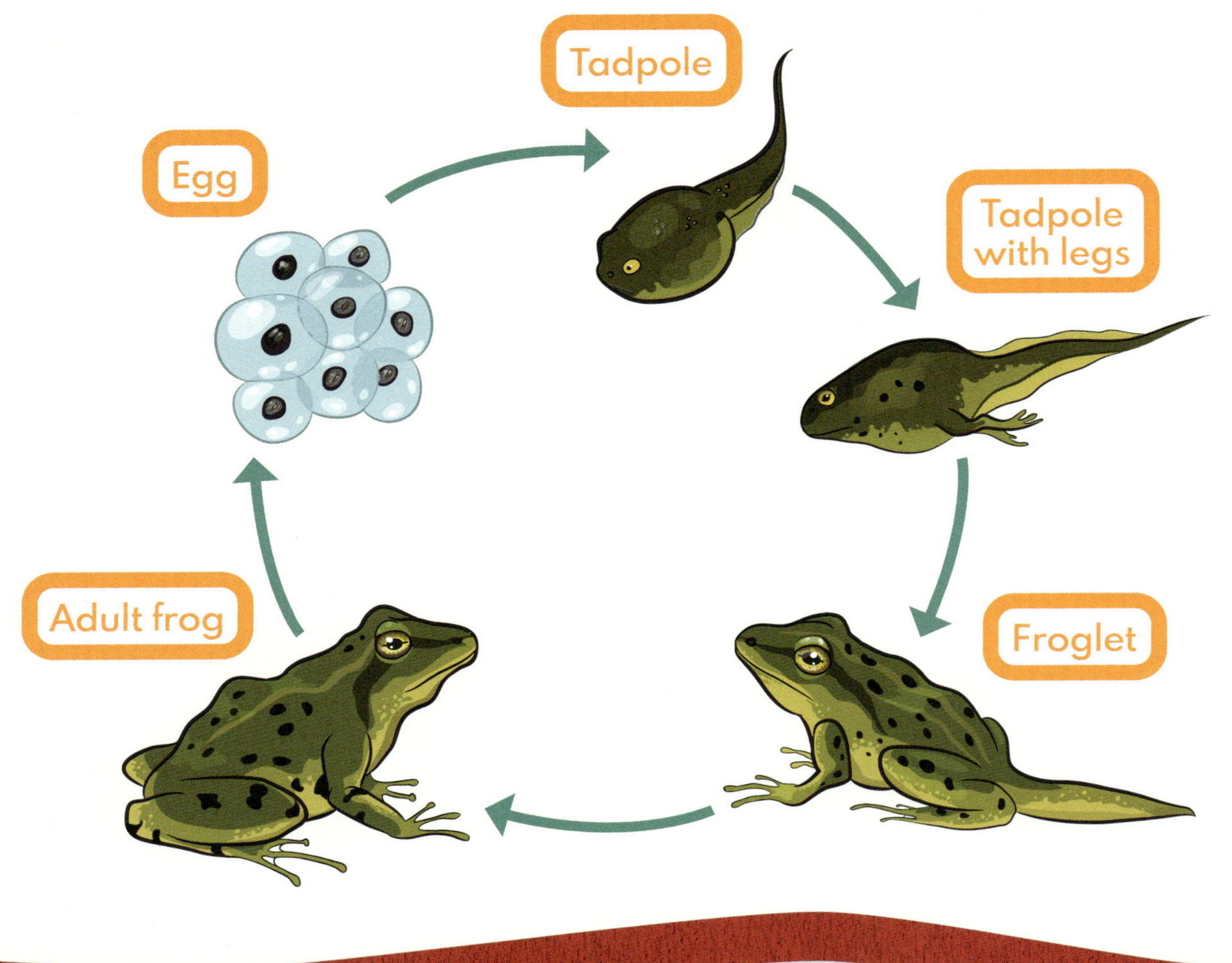

All living things go through a cycle of growing and reproducing. This is called a life cycle.

Scientists running the Vernal Pool Project use this data. They organize it and share it with local leaders. The leaders may consider this data when making decisions. The scientists also use the data to create a map of vernal pools in southwestern New Hampshire. They keep this map updated on the project's website. Visitors to the website can click on the locations of pools on the map. This shows them volunteer data about the pools.

Further Evidence

Look at the website below. Does it give any new evidence to support Chapter Two?

What Are Vernal Pools?

abdocorelibrary.com/amphibian-projects

There are more than 700 species of salamanders in the world.

Helping Salamanders Travel

Salamanders are common amphibians in some habitats. Many salamander species spend part of their lives in vernal pools. Some travel to the pools to **breed**.

This **migration** happens at the same time every year.

It is during the first warm, wet nights of spring. At that time, salamanders and other amphibians go looking for pools. However, these nights can be dangerous for salamanders. Busy roads may stand between them and vernal pools. Cars may even run over salamanders.

A citizen science project in New Hampshire helps local salamanders. The project is called

Effects of Roads on Wildlife

Roadkill is a clear example of how roads affect wildlife. But roads create other challenges too. Roads can split habitats into multiple pieces. Individual pieces may not be able to support living things that need lots of space. Noisy roads can harm animals that use sound to hunt and breed.

In some areas, people put up signs to warn drivers about amphibian crossings.

Salamander Crossing Brigades. On nights when many crossings are expected, volunteers meet at roads throughout the state. Kids can go with trusted adults. To stay safe, they wear reflective clothing. They stay off roads when cars are near.

And they do not stop traffic. But when it is safe to do so, volunteers help salamanders cross the road. They pick them up and carry them across.

Volunteers also collect data in this project. They count the living salamanders they see. And they even record the number of dead salamanders on the road. They send this data to the scientists running the project. The scientists

Volunteers should handle salamanders very carefully when helping them cross roads.

use it to learn where salamanders like to cross. Then they know where to send volunteers next year.

Amphibian Diseases

Human activity is not the only thing that threatens amphibians. Deadly diseases can spread among amphibians quickly. Experts want to know when this is happening. Sometimes they need to take action to help an area's amphibians survive.

Herpetofaunal Disease Alert System (HDAS) is a citizen science project in the United States and Canada. It helps inform experts about the spread of amphibian diseases. Volunteers keep an eye out in their areas.

School groups sometimes visit ponds and marshes on field trips. Students may spot diseased amphibians there.

They look for sick or dead amphibians. If they find one, they take pictures. They also write down the date and location. Then they send this information by email to project scientists.

Researchers can learn how far diseases have spread.

Citizen science projects give everyone the chance to contribute to scientific research. Projects on everything from space to plants to animals help experts learn more. People who love amphibians can find many ways to help out through amphibian projects.

Explore Online

Visit the website below. Does it give any new information about salamanders that wasn't in Chapter Three?

Salamander and Newt

abdocorelibrary.com/amphibian-projects

Science Projects

People recording frog mating calls need to travel to a frog habitat. They must be able to record their data and upload it online.

People studying vernal pools must be able to find and identify these pools.

People identifying amphibians should know what certain amphibians look like and be able to tell them apart.

People reporting sick or dead amphibians need to be able to email their data to project scientists.

Glossary

breed
to form a pair and have babies

data
information

habitat
the natural environment where a plant or animal lives

herpetofaunal
relating to amphibians and reptiles

mating calls
sounds that animals make to find partners for mating

migration
the regular movement of animals from one place to another

thrive
to grow well

Online Resources

To learn more about amphibian projects, visit our free resource websites below.

Visit **abdocorelibrary.com** or scan this QR code for free Common Core resources for teachers and students, including vetted activities, multimedia, and booklinks, for deeper subject comprehension.

Visit **abdobooklinks.com** or scan this QR code for free additional online weblinks for further learning. These links are routinely monitored and updated to provide the most current information available.

Learn More

Bell, Samantha S. *Animal Migration.* Abdo, 2026.

Vonder Brink, Tracy. *Amphibian Life Cycle.* Seahorse, 2022.

Vonder Brink, Tracy. *Amphibians.* Crabtree, 2023.

Index

About the Author

Ib Larsen is a writer and an editorial assistant living in Saint Paul, Minnesota.